9.95

MAR 2

WORDS

A book about the origins of everyday words and phrases

Text copyright © 1981 Jane Sarnoff
Illustrations copyright © 1981 Reynold Ruffins

Library of Congress Cataloging in Publication Data

Sarnoff, Jane.
Words: a book about the origins of everyday words and phrases.
Includes index.

SUMMARY: Traces the origin of common American-English words and phrases.
Also explains how the English language developed and words are formed.
1. English language—Etymology—Juvenile literature.
[1. English language—Etymology] I. Ruffins, Reynold. II. Title.
PE1574.S27   422   81-8943   ISBN 0-684-16958-4   AACR2

1 3 5 7 9 11 13 15 17 19 QD/C 20 18 16 14 12 10 8 6 4 2

Printed in the United States of America

WORDS

**A book
about the origins
of everyday
words and phrases**

By
Jane Sarnoff
and
Reynold Ruffins

Charles Scribner's Sons, New York

With thanks to, and appreciation of,
The Oxford English Dictionary and its *Supplements*
The Oxford Dictionary of English Etymology
The Random House Dictionary of the English Language
Brewer's Dictionary of Phrase and Fable
Fowler's Modern English Usage, 2nd ed.
(especially the entry of *irrelevant*)
Webster's New Collegiate Dictionary
The Romance of Names, Ernest Weekley,
E. P. Dutton & Company, New York, 1914
The American Language, H. L. Mencken,
Alfred A. Knopf, New York, 1963, and
Supplements One and Two
The Story of Language, Mario Pei,
J. B. Lippincott Company, Philadelphia, 1965
Verbatim, The Language Quarterly
Peggy Levin, of the New York Society Library

Pass the word...

In 55 BCE, a Roman general, Julius Caesar, conquered an island off the coast of Europe. The island, which Caesar named *Britain*, was the home of the Celts. The language they spoke, Celtic, was the old form of the languages still spoken in parts of Ireland, Scotland, and Wales. Many Celtic given names (see pages 27–31) are still used in English, as are a few Celtic words including *lad, dagger, kick, creak,* and *bun.*

Roman soldiers were stationed in Britain for four hundred years, but they never really settled there. They never brought their families or built homes outside army camps or mixed with the Celts. When the Romans left Britain, the few words of their Latin language left behind were about army life. The Latin for 'small fort', for example, is *castellum,* which became the English *castle.*

With no Roman army to protect them, the rich farms and fields of the Celts were invaded by Norsemen, Danes, and Picts. The Celts asked for help from the Germanic tribes who lived across the North Sea, the Angles and the Saxons. But the Celts got more help than they wanted: Within two hundred years there were more Angles and Saxons in Britain than there were Celts. The Celts were pushed back toward the northern and western edges of the island, taking most of their language with them.

The Angles and the Saxons spoke two slightly different Old Germanic languages and these, with a few Celtic and Latin words, were the start of the English we speak today. The Anglo-Saxon language was made up of short, simple words. Many of the words the Angles and the Saxons spoke when they arrived in Britain are still used today: *farm, sword, field, food, home, bread, house, floor, roof, oats, milk.*

Then, like all languages, the Anglo-Saxons' language began to change. New words were added for plants, buildings, objects, and customs that had not existed in the old country. Angle and Saxon words combined to make new words, pronunciation changed, old words were used in new ways. The changing language was given its first written form by traveling Christian monks, who named it after the Angles, *Anglish*—English. Because early English is so different from the English now spoken, it is called Old English. Other languages—Latin, German, French—also have early forms called "Old—".

In the 800s, Norsemen, people we also call the Vikings, sailed to Britain and settled there. They spoke Old Norse, a language related to the languages spoken today in Norway, Sweden, and Denmark. The Norsemen did not come in great numbers as the Angles and the Saxons had, but they brought their language and gave some words to English. *Ugly* and *fellow* come from the Old Norse, as do *sky, skin, skid, ski,* and most other English words that start with "sk".

In 1066, William of Normandy crossed the narrow waterway between Britain and Europe and conquered the Anglo-Saxons. The language William and his Norman people spoke was a type of Old French. Unlike the conquering Romans, many Normans settled in Britain. They became the nobles of the country. The French they spoke was the language of the court, the army, the universities, and the big cities. But in the small towns—and most of the English people lived in small towns—the people kept on speaking English. The stubborn Anglo-Saxons refused to learn the new king's language and would not even speak the few words they knew. For nearly a hundred years the two languages, Old English and Old French, were spoken side by side. The first French words to enter English were those that had not been necessary in English before the French arrived. The French introduced business terms such as *price, cash, expense;* family words such as *niece, nephew, cousin;* and words about the household such as *fork, dinner* (see Pig and Pork, page 45), *cushion, curtain,* and *dance.* Then, as more and more French words entered English, the language changed enough to become what we now call Middle English. Still, the language was definitely English. The Normans had beaten the Anglo-Saxons in battle, but in language the Anglo-Saxons had won: French was swallowed by English.

Because French is a modern form of Latin, many Latin-based words came into English with French. And then, starting in about 1400, Latin came directly into English.

Latin had become the international language of the church and of scholars. Most books were written in Latin, and Latin was used in the law courts and in the courts of the kings. Greek too was spoken by scholars, and the ancient Greek literature was again becoming popular. While Anglo-Saxon and old French words were simple, Latin and Greek words had many syllables. They were built of roots, prefixes, and suffixes (see Glossary, pages 60–61). They were complicated words, but life in Britain was becoming more complicated. People were traveling more; more books were being written; ideas were spreading quickly. Some ideas were easier to talk about using Greek and Latin words, and these words became part of English. Another language spoken by scholars was Hebrew, but few Hebrew words entered the language, except as given names (see pages 27–31).

By 1500, if you listened in on a conversation in England, with a bit of puzzling you could understand much of what was said. We call the language spoken then Modern English, our English. Of course, there were still many changes to come: changes in meaning, pronunciation, and especially in spelling. And many new words were yet to become English. In Shakespeare's time, the late 1500s, there were about 200,000 English words. Now there are more than 600,000. Some of the words developed to fill new needs, to describe new inventions, to express new ideas. Many new words entered the language when the colonists, who carried English to the New World, met with Dutch, Spanish, French, and Native American peoples and languages. Wherever English-speaking people live, work, play, or even fight with people who speak other languages, new words enter English. English is always growing, always changing.

Of the 600,000 words that now make up the English language, the average English-speaking adult knows about 15,000. But 99 percent of our everyday speech is made up of 1600 words. All of these words have stories—how *down* became *down* and *up, up* (see page 26); why an *umpire* is called that (see page 37); and why your name is what it is (see pages 27–31). Some words have changed their meaning completely over the centuries (see Nice, page 19); some have not changed at all (see Elbow, page 33). This book is a collection of our favorite word stories, some serious, some silly.* If you want to know about more word origins than are in this book, look in your library card catalogue under English Language—Etymology. (*Etymology* means the origin and development of a word; it is formed from two Greek words, *etumon,* 'true word', and *lögia,* 'study of'.)

*Kangaroos got their name in a really silly way. Captain Smith went exploring in Australia. He asked his guide the name of a large jumping animal. "Kangaroo," said the guide, and we have called that animal kangaroo ever since. But in the guide's language, *kangaroo* means 'I don't know'.

THE FAMILY

Mama, Papa, Baby

The first sounds an infant makes are *ma, pa* or *da,* and *ba.* In almost all languages these sounds, changed only a little, are taught to the child as words for its mother, *mama,* its father, *papa* or *dada,* and itself, *baba.*

Mama gave us the shortened form *ma* and also the British-English *mum* and *mummy,* and the American-English *mom* and *mommy.* From *papa* came *pa, poppa,* and the later slang *pop.* From *dada* came *dad* and *daddy. Baba* was used in English only until the 11th century. Then the word took two forms: *babe* for formal use—as in "babe in the manger" or "babe in arms"—and *baby* for everyday use.

Child

Child, a young human being, has been a word in English as long as English has been a language. And *child* seems to be only an English word; no trace of it can be found in other languages. At first spelled *cild,* the word meant the young of a highborn family, but it quickly came to mean all human young. The plural of *child* was *childre* or *childrer* until the end of the 12th century, when *children* became the usual pronunciation and spelling.

Boy

Boy came to Middle English as *boie, boye, beye, bye,* and sometimes even *bwey,* meaning 'a male servant' or 'a youth or man of low birth'. The Old French word from which *boy* came was *embiue,* which meant 'bindings' or 'a person who is tied up', 'a servant or a slave'. The Old French word came from a Latin word, which also meant 'bindings', and the Latin word came from a Greek word, pronounced *boeia,* which meant 'ox hide straps'. Not until the 14th century in England did *boy* come to mean a young male child, whether or not he was a servant. *Boy* is still used as an insult to an adult male thought to be of low birth or importance.

Girl

The German *gor* entered Middle English as *gurle, gerle,* or *girle,* meaning a child of either sex. Male children were often called *gurles* or *knave-gurles* until the 14th century, when *boy* (see above) took the meaning it now has. Not until the 16th century, however, was *girl* always used to mean a female child.

Husband

Husband is a combination of an Old English word, *hus,* from which we get the word *house,* and an Old Norse word, *bondi,* 'owner'. So a husband was a houseowner. The word was first used for all men who owned houses or were head of the household and later for all married men.

Adolescent and Adult

An *adolescent,* 'a growing youth', and an *adult,* 'a grown-up', often seem very far apart, but both words came from the same Latin phrase. *Adolescent* entered English in the 15th century and *adult* in the 16th century, both from the French. The French words had their start in the Latin *ad alescere. Ad* means 'toward' and *alescere,* 'to grow'.

Man and Woman

In Old English, *mann* meant 'a human being', male or female. The words, often as prefixes (see Glossary, page 60), that told the sex of the *mann* were *wer-*, 'man', and *wif* or *wif-mann,* 'woman'. Before *wif* was used to mean 'woman', it meant 'a married female', as it continues to mean today in our word *wife.*

Wer- is still used in *werewolf* (see page 53). And our word *world* is an Old English combination of *wer-* and *eld*, 'age': *wer-eld,* 'the age of mankind'. At first *world* meant not only the earth but also all of the time, the age, that mankind and human society had existed.

By the late 12th century, *man* was used for the male as well as for all mankind, and *wif-mann* for the female. The spelling* of *wif-mann* changed to *wiman, woman,* or *wuman.*

---

*Spelling is the way we write the sounds we hear. In most languages the spoken sounds are almost always written in the same way, and each written letter is almost always pronounced in the same way. But not in English. English pronunciation and spelling are weird; they don't match. In English almost every word, every combination of sounds, has its own rules. The consonants are bad enough, but the vowels are terrible. English has five written vowels—a,e,i,o,u—and these five letters are used to represent about forty-five sounds. In English, by pronunciation, fish could be spelled *ghoti: gh* as in enough, *o* as in women, and *ti* as in nation.

During most of the time English has existed, few people could write the language. Those who could didn't think spelling was important; the important thing was understanding. (Shakespeare spelled his name five or six ways, including *Shagsper.*) In this book several different early spellings are sometimes given for the same word. All of those spellings were considered correct; a word was even spelled in different ways in the same book or letter.

People who wrote in English didn't begin to care about spelling until the mid-19th century. Scholars, dictionary makers, and educators then started to make rules about which spelling of a word was correct, but they paid little attention to matching the spoken sound of English with the written word. And so today it's hard to write English correctly. But (butt) do (dew, due) not (knot) be (bee) so (sew, sow) blue (blew). For (fore, four) wait (weight)! Who (hoo) knows (noes, nose)? Some (sum) days (daze) what (watt) we (wee) hear (here) we'll (wheel) write (right) right (write).

Bride and Bridal

Bride came to English from an Old German word meaning 'to cook' or 'to make broth'. The first job given to a new daughter-in-law in a family might have been to make the broths necessary for the daily meals. *Bridal*—used to describe a wedding party—is an Old English combination of *bride* and *ale,* the drink. A lot of ale drinking was done at the bride party.

Wed

In the 12th century, a man and a woman could *wed*—spelled *wedden.* But someone could also *wedden* on a horse or a cockfight. Or a person who had no money could *wedden* a silver ring at a pawn broker. In Old English, *wedden* meant to 'pledge', 'pawn', or 'bet'. By the end of the 13th century, the meaning 'pledge' became used most often, and that's what we do now when we wed—we pledge ourselves one to the other.

Gossip

Gossip comes from the Old English *godsibb,* 'godparent'. *Godsibb* came from the word *god* plus *sibb,* a word used to show a close relationship. Our word *siblings,* meaning 'brothers or sisters of the same parents', comes from the same word.

Of course, godparents, *godsibbs,* were people you knew well enough to talk openly with, to tell all your secrets to. So, over the centuries, the word *godsibb,* or *gossip,* came to be used for a person you could talk to easily. By Shakespeare's time, a gossip was a person who talked too much, too easily, and who told secrets, just as a gossip is today.

SHIPS AT SEA

Starboard, Port, Port, and Portholes

The right side of a ship, when you are facing forward, is called the *starboard*. The word is a combination of the Old English *steor*, 'rudder' or 'steer', and *bord*, meaning 'side'. The right side of the ship was the side on which the rudder was fastened.

The left side of the ship was called the *larboard*. *Lar* probably comes from the Old English word *lade* or *load*. The larboard was the side of the ship from which the ship was loaded. (It wasn't possible to load the ship from the starboard because the rudder would get in the way.) But *larboard* and *starboard* sound so much alike—especially during a storm with the wind blowing—that for safety's sake, the left side was often called the *port* side. The word *port* was used because the larboard was the side of the ship toward the port or harbor when the boat was being loaded.

The word *port*, meaning 'harbor', comes from the Latin word *portus*, 'a safe place' or 'haven'. But the *port* in *portholes* comes from the Latin word *porta*, meaning 'door'.

Spinning a yarn

When we *spin a yarn* we tell a story. But the expression started with sailors sitting on the deck of a ship repairing ropes. A rope—called a *yarn*—often needed smaller pieces of yarn braided onto its end. The braiding or winding was called *spinning*. And so the work was called *spinning a yarn*. To pass the time, the sailors told stories while they worked, and *spinning a yarn* was soon used about the stories rather than the work.

Flotsam and Jetsam

Parts of wrecked ships, old bottles, life jackets, and other things found floating in the sea are called *flotsam and jetsam.* The word *flotsam* comes from the Old French *floter,* meaning 'to float'. The word *jetsam* comes from the French *jeter,* meaning 'to throw out'.

Scuba

The word *scuba,* the name of equipment used for breathing underwater, comes from the initials* of *S*elf-*C*ontained-*U*nderwater *B*reathing *A*pparatus.

Siren

Siren, which now means a noise or alarm or warning, comes from the Greek word *seiren.* In Greek mythology, the Sirens were birdlike creatures that had the head, breasts, and arms of women. The Sirens sat on rocks in the sea and sang to call sailors to them—and to a shipwreck on the rocks. Certainly, anyone hearing the Sirens would be warned or alarmed.

SOS and Posh

Often we hear stories about the origin of words that sound great, but just aren't true. Among them are stories about the origins of *SOS* and *posh.*

SOS, the emergency call used at sea, is not the acronym* for *S*ave *O*ur *S*hip. The Morse code message—three short beeps, three long, and three short—was chosen because it is easy to send and understand. It doesn't stand for anything.

Posh means 'really fancy or grand', 'the best'. The word is said to have started in the days of steamship travel between England and India. Because of the position of the sun, the most comfortable cabins were on the port side of the ship on the trip out and the starboard on the trip home. *P*ort *O*ut, *S*tarboard *H*ome —POSH—was said to be written on the reservations of passengers who could afford the best. But *posh,* with the same meaning it has today, was used in English before there was regular travel between England and India.

*A word made from the initial letters of other words is called an *acronym.*

FRIENDS AND ENEMIES

Friend

In the 11th century a *friend* was a family member. Then, most households had two groups of people: the family, or those beloved of the householder, and the slaves. The Old German, and later the Old English, word for 'a relative', 'a beloved one', was *freond*. In English, *freond* was soon spelled *freend* or *friend* and meant anyone who was loved or cared about. The Old German word for the entire group of beloved ones—all those who were not slaves—was *frei*. In English *frei* changed in spelling to *free*, and the meaning slowly changed from 'beloved ones' to 'not slaves'—free.

Enemy

Enemy came to English from two Latin words. The prefix (*see* Glossary, page 60) *in-*, later changed to *en-*, means 'not'. The root word (*see* Glossary, page 60) *amicus* means 'friend'. An enemy is not a friend. *Enemy*, spelled just as we spell it, has been part of English since the late 1200s—quite a record for a language as changeable as English.

Pal

Our word *pal* came directly from the Romney (language of the gypsies) word *plal*, meaning 'friend', 'brother', 'comrade'. *Pal* sounds like a modern word, but it has been used in English since before the Pilgrims set sail for the New World.

Wet Blanket

A *wet blanket* is a person who takes all the fun and spirit out of things, who says "no" to every exciting plan. The expression comes from the use of a wet blanket or other heavy piece of cloth to put out fires, to smother the sparks.

Silly

Silly comes from the Old German word *selig*, meaning 'blessed'. When the word entered English as *seely* in the 12th century, it still meant 'blessed', but was used most often about the sort of person—said to have the Lord's blessing—who was simpleminded or without knowledge. Because such people were thought to be particularly happy, the word *seely* came to mean 'happy'. Then, because such happy people could be easily tricked, the word—which had changed in spelling to *selly* or *silly*—changed in meaning to 'simple', 'foolish', and 'not serious'.

Pipsqueak

In the 15th century, the Irish, or Celtic, word for apple was *pippen*. Throughout the British Isles, the word *pip* came to be used for the seed of an apple and, later, for the seed of any fruit, especially the seeds of oranges and lemons. In England a new expression "I'll squeeze you till the pips squeak" meant to squeeze someone like a lemon or an orange until the seeds could be heard. The expression soon turned into a single word, *pipsqueak*, meaning someone who complained under pressure. After a while, the word came to mean anyone who was small and whined about troubles.

Nice

Nice has a way of changing meaning. It came into English from the Old French in the 12th century meaning 'silly' or 'simple'. By the 13th century it meant 'foolish and stupid'. In the 14th century a nice person was one who was too free and open: A parent might tell a child "Don't be so nice." Then, in the 15th century, *nice* was turned around completely to mean 'shy'. By the 16th century and for about the next two hundred years, *nice* meant 'dainty', 'precise', and 'absolutely accurate'. The word was used more about things, facts, and thoughts than about people. In the middle of the 18th century, *nice* took on the meaning it has most often today. It is a complimentary word, used about people and things, meaning 'agreeable', 'pleasant', 'delightful'. But *nice* may soon be in for another change. We have used the word so often that it no longer sounds like a compliment. You can now call someone *nice* and make the word seem to mean 'just ok' or 'nothing special'.

Terrific

If you told an Englishman of the 17th century that he was terrific, he would wonder how he had frightened you. The Latin word *terrificus*, 'frightened', gave us the English word *terrific*, meaning—until very recently—'something that causes fear or terror'. Because anything that caused fear or terror was out of the ordinary, *terrific* soon took on the second meaning of extraordinary or unusual in a bad, frightening, or terrible way. Only during the last twenty-five years has terrific been turned around to mean something unusually good, outstanding, or magnificent.

Coward

The English word *coward* comes from the Latin word *cauda*, meaning 'tail'. The word was used to describe the tail of an animal running away when frightened, as in the expression "turning tail." The family name *Coward* has nothing to do with fear, but comes from the occupation of cowherd.

Crazy

In the 1500s an English sailor might complain that his boat was crazy and could easily sink. Or a housewife might say her bowl was too crazy to hold water. Then, *crazy* meant 'full of cracks'. It was not until the 17th century that *cracked* or *crazy* was used about people. Someone who seemed odd or different might be called a crackbrain or a crazybrain. In the late 17th century, *crazy* and *cracked* were both used to mean 'insane', 'of unsound mind'. Both words have almost always been used as insults, rather than as serious terms for those with mental problems.

Fool

Fool came into English in the 13th century, by way of the Old French, from the Latin *follis*. The Latin word means 'a bellows', 'a blown-up ball', or 'a windbag'; but in English the word *fool* has always been an insult. Like a windbag or a balloon when the air is suddenly let out, a fool makes a lot of noise, but says little that makes sense. Today we not only have the word *fool* but we also call a person who talks too much and says too little a *windbag*.

Shirt and Skirt

An Old German word *shurt*, 'short', gave Old English the word *scyrte*. In some parts of England *scyrte* meant 'an undergarment for the top of the body', in other parts it meant 'a part of a dress from the waist down', and in some places it meant both. Since neither a shirt nor a skirt are the whole dress, both could be called 'short' parts. In the late part of the 13th century, the word divided into *shirt* and *skirt*—with much the same meanings they have now. No one is sure what caused this division of the word, but it must have gotten rid of a lot of confusion when the Old English were getting dressed.

Denim

Denim, the material we make blue jeans from, was first used in England in the 1600s. It was called *serge*, a type of cloth, *de Nîmes*, 'from Nimes', the town in France where the cloth was made. The term was first shortened to *de Nîmes*, and then to *denim*.

Dungarees

In the 17th century, English sailors in the Eastern seas used an especially strong Indian cloth to make new sails for their ships and pants for themselves. The Indians, who spoke the Hindi language, called the cloth *dungari*. The English spelled the word *dungaree* and used it most often to mean the pants which they made from the cloth.

Galoshes

Galoshes are rubber or plastic overshoes worn to keep our regular shoes dry. When we got the word in English, from the Old French, *galoche* were wooden sandals worn to protect fancy shoes from the mud. The French got the word originally from the Latin *gallicula*. And that's really strange because the Latin word came from France! When the Roman army marched into France—or Gaul, as they called it—they saw the Gaulish, or Gallic, people wearing strange wooden sandals. The Romans called the sandals *gallicula*, putting together the Latin word for France and the Latin word for sandals. So the French took from the Romans a Latin word meaning 'French sandals'. No one knows what the French called the sandals before the Romans arrived.

Kerchief

The word for a piece of cloth that covers the head—a *kerchief*—came to Middle English in the 12th century from two Old French words: *couvrir,* 'cover' and *chief,* 'head'. *Chief,* meaning 'leader' or 'head person', came to English from the same French word. And so did the English/French word *chef,* or 'cook', which really means 'head of the kitchen'.

Umbrella

Umbrella comes from the Latin word *umbra,* 'shade'. In the sunnier parts of the world, especially in the East, umbrellas were used to make shade, to protect the user from the heat of the sun. Umbrellas were first used in London for protection against the heavy rains of the spring of 1750 by Jonas Hanway, who had traveled to the East. People laughed at Hanway, but the umbrella soon became popular in damp London and then throughout the world.

Pocket, a Pig in a Poke, Let the Cat out of the Bag

A *poke* in Middle English was a bag; a *poket* was a small bag (see Diminutive, page 61). When a *poket*, later spelled *pocket*, was sewn into clothing, there was no reason to give it a new name—it was still a small bag.

Miners in the California Gold Rush days talked about their *poke*, meaning the gold they had in their bags. But the word *poke* is used in English today more often in the expression "to buy a pig in a poke," meaning to buy something unseen. A book written in England in 1580 tells how thieves would try to cheat people by putting a cat in a closed poke and pretending it was a pig. If the bag were opened and the cat escaped, the buyers were said to have "let the cat out of the poke." We now say "let the cat out of the bag," meaning let the truth be seen or let the facts be known.

Pea jacket

When you say you are going to wear a pea jacket, you are really saying a 'jacket jacket'. *Pij* was the Dutch word for a heavy cloth jacket their sailors wore in the 1700s. When the English sailors in the colonies asked the Dutch what the piece of clothing was called, the Dutch said *"Pij,"* pronounced *pea*. And so the English called the jacket a *pij jacket*—a jacket jacket. *Jacket* came to English from the Old French *jaquet*, meaning a 'little *jaque*' or 'coat' (see Diminutive, p. 61). Where the *jaque* first came from is not certain. It may have first meant the leather "coating" around a clay or metal container for liquid and then the leather coat that went over armor.

Thinking Cap

Now when we say "I must put on my thinking cap," we mean we are going to think about something very carefully. But long ago a thinking cap was a real hat. In England judges put on a special cap—a *thinking cap*—while sentencing a criminal to death, as a sign that they had thought carefully about the punishment.

Corduroy

The story—believed to this day—is that corduroy was invented for the kings of France to wear while hunting. For hundreds of years, common people were not supposed to wear the material. The name was said to come from the French words *corde de roi*, 'cloth of the king'. That's what the name means, but the name, the cloth, and the story were made up by English weavers in the 1700s. The weavers hoped the story would help sell the material, and it did— even to the French, who thought the kings in the story were English kings.

Perfume

Perfume came to English, through the Italian, from the Latin. The prefix (*see* Glossary, page 60) *per-* is used in its meaning of 'through, or by means of'. The root (*see* Glossary, page 60) comes from the Latin *fumus*, 'smoke'. In ancient times incense, flowers, and other sweet things were burnt during religious ceremonies. The ceremonies often included bad-smelling events such as the killing and burning of a sacrifice—a bird or larger animal. The smell was covered up *per fumus*—through, or by means of, the smoke from the incense.

Purple

The English word *purple* goes back to Latin. The Roman emperors and their families wore white togas trimmed with dark red to show their royal rank. The color, made from berries which were difficult to find, washed out easily. But for many years there was no other way to make the dye. Finally a long-lasting dye of the right color was made by crushing and boiling the shell of a lobsterlike fish from the coast of North Africa. The name of the shellfish, and so of the color, was *pupura*.

ON THE MOVE

Automobile

Auto- is a Greek prefix (see Glossary, page 60) which means 'self' or 'by oneself'. *Mobile* means 'moveable'. *Mobile* came to English in the 15th century, through the French, from the Latin word *movere*, 'to move'. The two words were put together in the United States in 1887 to give a name to a new invention. The invention was a carriage that moved by itself, using a motor, without needing a horse to pull it—an automobile.

Car

Car has meant a 'wheeled vehicle' for carrying people and things since the middle of the 14th century. The word came to English from the Old Dutch as *carre*, but it can be traced back through the centuries to the Latin *currus*, 'chariot'.

Bus

A *bus* is a large vehicle that carries many people as part of a public transportation system. In 1828 the French put such a vehicle into use for the first time and needed to give it a name. They called it an *omnibus*, the Latin word meaning 'for all', because anyone could ride on it. The next year the English used the word *omnibus* for their public carriages. By 1875 *bus* was English slang for *omnibus*, but by 1900 *bus* was considered standard English.

Up and Down

Up comes from the Old English *upp* or *uppe*. Although the word has long had its present meaning, in the earliest English *uppe* meant 'of the heavens' or 'toward the heavens'. And toward the heavens, of course, was up.

Down was first *afdown* or *ofdune,* a combination of two Old English words. *Af* or *of* meant 'from'. *Down* or *dune* meant 'hill'. So *afdown*, soon shortened to *down*, meant 'off the hill'. And if you were off the hill, you were down.

Canter

In the 1600s it was the style in England to take a religious journey, called a pilgrimage, to sacred places. A pilgrimage to the town of Canterbury was a favorite trip because the roads were good and the countryside beautiful. The pilgrims rode their horses slowly, stopping often to look at views and to visit friends and relatives. The speed at which they rode their horses, a very slow and gentle gallop, was called the *Canterbury.* Later the term was shortened to the one we use today, *canter.*

Tote

Tote means 'to carry'. We use the word most often today in *totebag. Tote* was one of the many words given to English by Africans, brought as slaves to America in the 17th, 18th, and 19th centuries. The word was originally *tota*, meaning 'to carry', in the language spoken in the part of Africa from which the slaves were taken.

NAMES

Adam, from a Hebrew word used for either 'red earth' or 'man'. As a family name Adam(s).

Alan, Allan, Allen, from the Celtic probably meaning 'cheerful'. As a family name Alan(son).

Amy, through the French *Amée*, 'beloved', from the Latin for 'greatly loved'. As a family name Ames.

Barbara, from the Greek *barbaros* meaning 'foreign'.

Bradley, from the Old English 'from the broad meadow'. Used as a given or family name.

Carey, Cary, from the Celtic, meaning 'from the fortress'. The name, with many different spellings can be male or female, a given or family name.

Carter, from the Old English meaning 'cart driver'. Originally a family name, now also a given name.

Charles, Carol, Carroll, from the Old French meaning 'man'. All forms were originally male given names. In the early 19th century, **Carol** became a female name in the United States. All forms are now used as given and family names.

Daniel, Daniella, from the Hebrew 'God has judged'. As a family name Daniel(s).

David, perhaps from a Hebrew term of affection meaning 'darling' or 'beloved'.

Dolores, the Spanish for 'sorrowful'.

Earl, from the Anglo-Saxon for 'nobleman' or 'chief'. Originally a title or nickname, now a given or family name.

Elizabeth, from the Hebrew for 'God's promise'.

Eric, Erica, from the Norse meaning 'powerful', often used about rulers.

Frances, Francis, from a nickname meaning 'French'.

Franklin, from the Old German 'freeman'. Used originally as a family name, and later, often as **Frank,** a given name.

George, from the Greek for 'farmer'. Used as a given or family name.

Hamilton, from the Old French, 'from a mountain'. Originally a Scottish family name, now occasionally also a given name.

Helen, a pre-Greek name of unknown meaning, although often said to mean 'bright'. Many female names have, through the centuries, come from **Helen: Helena, Elaine,** possibly **Eleanora,** and **Ellen.**

Irving, from an early Scottish place name, possibly meaning 'sea gift'. Originally a family name, now also a given name.

Isabelle, the French form of **Elizabeth,** but also in French a yellowish-brown color.

James, from the Hebrew for 'the surplanter', the same Hebrew word as **Jacob.** Often used as a given name for a second son and as a family name. As a family name, also as Jam(ison).

Joanna, John, from the Hebrew for 'gift of God'. The female version of the name is also used as **Jane, Jean,** and **Joan.** As a family name often John(son) or John(s) or Joan(s), from which came our common family name Jones.

Judith, from the Hebrew for 'Jewish woman'.

Karen, the Scandinavian form of **Katherine,** which goes back to a Greek name with an unknown meaning. Other forms are **Catherine, Kate, Kathleen, Katrina,** and **Kay. Kitty** has been used as a nickname for all forms.

Kenneth, a Celtic given name meaning 'handsome'.

Laura, Laurence, Lawrence, from the Latin *laurus,* 'laurel, bay tree'.

Lawton, from the Old English 'from the hillside farm'. Originally a given name, now usually a family name.

Lee, from an Old English family name, **Leah,** meaning 'meadow, clearing'. Now used for male or female as a given or family name.

Lincoln, from the Old English for 'the settlement by the pool'. Originally a given name, now usually a family name.

Lisa, Lise, Liza, often said to be from **Elizabeth,** but possibly originally from the Hebrew 'sacred to God'.

Maxwell, from the Anglo-Saxon for 'dweller by the stream'. Originally a family name, occasionally used as a given name.

Melissa, from the Greek for 'honeybee'.

Michael, from the Hebrew 'who is like God?'. As a family name often Michael(s) and Michael(son). The female version is the modern French **Michelle.**

Miriam, found in Hebrew but probably originally Egyptian, has no known meaning. The more common name **Mary** came from the same Hebrew name.

Murray, from the Celtic for 'seaman'. Used as a given and family name.

Nancy, of uncertain origin, possibly from **Agnes** or **Anne,** the Hebrew for 'grace'.

Natalie, from the Latin for 'birthday'.

Newton, from the Anglo-Saxon meaning 'from the new place'. Used most often as a family name.

Oakley, from the Old English for 'from the oak tree meadow'. Used as a family name.

Pamela, a name made up by Sir Philip Sidney for a character in a book written in 1590.

Patricia, Patrick, from the Latin for 'noble'.

Peter, from the Greek for 'stone'. Originally a given name, now often a family name as in Peter(s) and Peter(son).

Philip, from the Greek for 'lover of horses'. As a family name Philip(s) and Philip(son).

Preston, from the Old English for 'from the priest's land'. Used as a given and family name.

Quincy, a family name from the name of several French villages, after a Roman soldier *Quintus,* 'fifth'.

Radcliffe, from the Old English for 'red cliff'. Once a given name, now a family name.

Reynold, Ronald, from the Anglo-Saxon *Regenwald*, a combination of two words meaning 'strength', which also gave rise to **Reginald.** As a family name usually Reynold(s) and Ronald(s).

Richard, from the Old German for 'stern but just'. Used as a given and family name. As a family name often Richard(s) and Richard(son).

Robert, Roberta, from the Old German for 'bright fame'. As a family name usually Robert(s) and Robert(son).

Scott, a family name for a person of Scottish origin, now generally used as a given name.

Smith, from the Old English for a craftsman, especially a worker in metals. Used as a family name, often with the addition of the metal, as in Goldsmith, or the location of the shop, as in Smithfield.

Standish, from the Old English for 'from the stony park'. Usually a family name.

Stanley, from the Old English for 'from the stony seaside'. Used as a given or family name.

Stephanie, Stephen, Steven, from the Greek for 'crown'. Used as a given or family name. As a family name often Stephen(s) or Stephen(son).

Susan, from the Hebrew for 'trusting', also used for the flower 'lily'.

Thomas, from the Aramaic, a common language in the time of Christ, meaning 'twin'. At first a nickname, later a given name, and then a family name.

Thurston, from the Scandinavian for 'Thor's stone'. Used as a given or a family name.

Truman, from the Old English for 'loyal man'. Occasionally a given name, but most often a family name.

Upton, from the Anglo-Saxon for 'from the high town'. Used as a given or family name.

Vandam, from the Dutch for 'from the dike'. Used as a family name.

Vera, from the Russian for 'faith'.

Racket

The games we call *racket* sports—tennis, ping pong, racket ball, squash—all began with a game in which a ball was hit with the palm of the hand. Our English word *racket* came from the Arabic word *rahat,* meaning 'palm of the hand'. The word came to English, from the French *raquette,* in the 16th century.

Marathon

In 490 BCE, the Athenians defeated the Persians in battle at a place called Marathon. A Greek runner carried the news of the battle to the city of Athens, 26.6 miles away. Today, in honor of that runner, we have special races, called *marathons,* that are 26.6 miles long.

Race

When *race* first came to English from the Old Norse in the 13th century, it meant 'a rush of water' or 'a quickly moving stream'. In the 14th century *race* kept this meaning, but could also mean the rushing of people or animals. During the next two centuries, *race* came to have its present meaning of 'rushing' or 'running', especially in competition with others.

Speed

Speed entered Old English, from the German, as *spedan,* meaning 'do well' or 'succeed'. The original meaning is still heard in England when a traveler is wished *good speed,* meaning 'have a good trip', or 'good luck'—not 'go fast'. Through the years, because the word *speed* was often used to wish well to someone going on a trip, its meaning changed slowly to wishing that the person would come out ahead of others, go farther, move faster. And faster. And faster. Speed.

Amateur

An *amateur* plays a game or studies a subject for love, not money. Olympic athletes are amateurs; major league ball players are professionals who play for money. The word *amateur* comes from the Latin word *amare,* 'to love'.

Target

Target, something to aim or fire at, came into English in the 14th century from France. Throughout Europe, foot soldiers protected themselves from enemy lances and arrows with a shield, a round metal plate. During peacetime, the shield, called a *targe* in French, was nailed to a post to give soldiers practice with their lances. The *targe* was made smaller and circles were drawn around it to make the practice harder. The smaller *targe* was called a *targette,* or a 'small shield' (see Diminutive, page 61).

Umpire

In Old French, a man who was called in to settle an argument between two others was called *a noumpere*. The word was a combination of two Latin words: *non*, meaning 'not', and *par*, meaning 'equal' or 'the same'. The man who made the decision was not the same as the other men. The 15th-century English, hearing *a noumpere*, incorrectly divided the French words to sound better to English ears. The English wrote the word *an umpere* or, as now, *an umpire*. The same type of incorrect division gave us *an apron* which had been *a napron*, 'a small cloth'.

Bleachers

At a baseball field, the inexpensive seats are called the *bleachers*. The word *bleach* means 'to lighten' as the sun can lighten things. When baseball first started, the only seats were benches in the sun. Because the benches were always in the sun they became lighter in color and were called *bleaches* or *bleachers*.

Dodgers

When the *Dodgers* first started as a baseball team, in Brooklyn, New York, they were called the Brooklyn Robins. In those days, the 1920s, there were few buses and no subways in Brooklyn, but there were a lot of trolley cars. In fact, there were so many trolleys and their drivers were so careless that the nickname for people from Brooklyn became the *trolley dodgers*. The Brooklyn Robins took the name *Dodgers*, too, and kept it even after they dodged out of Brooklyn to Los Angeles.

Park

In French the word *parc* first meant 'a herd of animals'. When *parc* entered English in the 13th century, it meant 'an enclosed area of land owned by the royal family, where animals could be kept and hunted'. By the middle of the 16th century, a *park* had become any enclosed land set aside not just for hunting but for all types of pleasure and recreation.

Canoe

When early Spanish explorers sailed to Haiti, the people who lived there met them in boats made of hollowed-out logs. The name for the boats, *canoa,* was taken directly into Spanish. When the Spanish settled on the southeastern coast of America, they passed the word *canoa* to the French settlers, who changed the spelling to *canoe.* The French settlers passed the word to the English settlers, who kept the spelling but said the word as if it were spelled *canoo.* The Native American peoples who used such boats before the arrival of the Europeans had had very different names for their boats, but they picked up the word *canoe* from the French, Spanish, and British settlers.

MONEY

In Rome, in 344 BCE, a temple was built in honor of the
goddess Juno, who had warned the city of an invading army.
The temple was named for *Juno Moneta*, 'Juno who warns'.
Built into the temple, and under the protection of the
goddess and her priests, was the first Roman mint—the
place where precious metals were turned into coins. The
word *moneta* was used for the mint and the coins made
there, as well as for the temple. Later *moneta* was used for
all coins, no matter where they were minted. The word
money, as *monei* or *mone*, has been used in English since
the 1300s.

Salary

Soldiers in the Roman army were not paid in money.
Instead, they were given food, clothing, and other things
necessary for life. Each month, however, the soldiers were
paid a few coins with which to buy especially important
things, particularly salt, *sal* in Latin. The money was called
salarium, meaning 'salt ration'. In the 14th century, the word
entered English, through the Old French, as *salarie*,
meaning 'money paid for doing a regular job'.

Dollar
Dollar comes from a German word *Thaler,* which was short for *Joachimsthal. Joachimsthal* is the name of an area of Germany where silver, used in making coins, was mined. The word has been used in English for a unit of money since 1519.

Buck
No one is too sure how a dollar came to be called a *buck,* but it may have happened first in a poker game in the American West. In the 1850s, a marker, called a *buck* for unknown reasons, was put in front of the man who was to deal next. The marker was usually a silver dollar. It's possible that *buck* then came to be used not just for the marker but for all silver dollars and then for paper dollars. Perhaps this was even the beginning of our expression "to pass the buck," meaning 'to pass the responsibility'. *Buck* has been part of the English language for 150 years, but it is still considered slang.*

Genuine
The English word *genuine* means 'real' or 'not counterfeit'. The word came to English from the French word *genu,* meaning 'knee', which came from the earlier Latin word for knee. But what's the connection between *real* and *knee?* The two words came together in an old custom in which the father of a newborn child placed the infant on his knee as a way of accepting the child as his real son or daughter.

Nickel
Nickels, our five-cent coins, were first made out of a metal called nickel.

Bank
The word *bank,* a place where money is kept and exchanged, came to English from medieval Italy. The Italian moneylenders did their work at narrow benches called *bancas.*

*Almost 10% of the words we use every day are considered slang. That's more than in many other languages, which adds to the problems of learning English as a foreign language.

Boss

Boss was brought to English in the United States by Dutch settlers in the 1800s. *Baas* was the Dutch word for 'master'. In earlier Dutch, the word was a term of respect for an older male relative or family friend, as we might now use the word *uncle*. Even earlier, *baas* was a German word of respect for an older female relative, a cousin or an aunt.

Carat

The weight of diamonds, rubies, and other precious gems is measured in *carats*. The word comes from *carob*, the Arabic name for a tree with seed pods that all weigh almost exactly the same. The seeds were used in the ancient bazaars of Africa to balance the scales when the gems were weighed.

Skinflint

When the English of the 1700s wanted to describe someone who was very stingy with money and drove hard bargains, they would say "he could skin a flint." The French said "he could skin an egg." Of course, neither flints, a type of stone, nor eggs can be skinned. The expressions meant to take something where there is nothing—and the person who could do this was called a *skinflint*.

White Elephant

In Siam, white elephants were considered sacred and were not supposed to be put to work. When the king of Siam wanted to ruin someone, he gave that person a gift of a white elephant. The elephant was expensive to feed and care for, but could not be made to work for its keep. Today we use the phrase *white elephant* about a possession that is not worth the expense or the care it needs.

MEALTIME

Belly, Stomach, and Throat

Belly is one of the oldest English words. It started in Old English as *belig*, meaning 'skin bag'. *Belig* was used for a type of skin bag used to carry or store such foods as beans and peas, and for the part of our body now usually called stomach. *Stomach* came from a Greek word meaning 'mouth' or 'opening'. In Old English it was usually used for one of our body openings, the part we now call our throat. Now and then *stomach* was used to mean the belly as well as the throat. In those days the word *throat,* which came from an Old German word meaning 'to push out', meant only the front part of a man's neck where his Adam's apple pushed out. (For Adam's apple, read your Bible.)

In the 1850s the English thought that *belly* was just a little too natural a word, so they used *stomach* instead as a euphemism (*see* White Meat and Dark Meat, page 44). *Stomach,* since it meant opening, didn't make as much sense as *belly,* but the English thought it sounded much more polite.

Turkey

Portuguese explorers of the 1500s brought to Europe birds they had found in New Guinea. The birds were called *turkeys* because when the explorers returned home, they traveled through the countries in which the Turks lived, and it was thought in Europe that the birds had been found there. When the first American colonists found similar birds, they called them *turkeys* too. Now the first turkeys are called *guinea fowl,* after the place they really came from, but the American birds are still misnamed *turkeys.*

White Meat and Dark Meat

Before the time of Queen Victoria of England, a person who wanted a leg, breast, or thigh of turkey or chicken just asked for it. But in the mid 1800s, people got very very prim and proper. And it was not considered proper to use any word related to the body, including *leg, breast,* or *thigh*— even when the body was that of a bird. Instead, polite people asked for *white meat* or *dark meat.*

Human legs were called *limbs.* So were the legs of tables, sofas, and chairs. Furniture was covered with cloths that reached the floor so that their limbs couldn't be seen. Even the word *chair* became too personal a word for ladies to use—they said *seat.* There was absolutely no polite word for the part of a body that sits on a seat.

Words used as substitutes for words thought to be improper, evil, or bad manners are called *euphemisms,* from the Greek word meaning 'good-sounding speech'.

Bread and Loaf

Bread and *loaf* are both Old English words that probably came from the Old German. In English before 1200, *loaf* meant 'bread'. And *bread* meant a 'piece or slice' of loaf or of anything else. In 1100, if you had wanted what we call a piece of bread, you would have said "Please give me a bread of loaf." As more and more people asked for a *bread,* the word came to mean the food; and *loaf* was used for the whole shaped and baked object.

Ketchup

Ketchup, the word and the sauce, sailed into England on the ships of 18th-century Dutch traders. The Dutch, who called the sauce *ketjap*, had gotten it from the Chinese, who called it *ketsiap*. *Ketsiap*, as made by the Chinese, was a spicy sauce of fish broth and black mushrooms eaten with rice. Tomatoes were added by the English to make the sauce less spicy and more to their own taste.

Mustard

To make *mustard*, the seed of a particular plant is ground very fine and mixed with a liquid. The Romans, who first made the mixture, used a new wine as the liquid. The wine, called *must* in Latin, meaning 'new' or 'fresh', gave its name to the mixture and to the plant from which the seed came.

Pig and Pork

On Anglo-Saxon farms there were animals called *pigs*,* *sheep*, and *cows*. When the Normans invaded England, they brought the Old French words for the same animals, words that became the English words *pork, mutton*, and *beef*. The Anglo-Saxons, who became servants to the Normans, continued to use their own words for the animals in the fields and barns where the Normans seldom went. But when the Anglo-Saxons worked in the Norman houses and kitchens, they used the Norman words. We now use the Anglo-Saxon words *pig, sheep*, and *cow* to speak of live animals and the Norman words *pork, mutton*, and *beef* to speak of the meat or flesh of these animals. We also use the Anglo-Saxon field words *calf* and *deer* and the Norman kitchen words *veal* and *venison*.

Filbert nut

Filbert nuts were named after St. Philbert, whose feast day fell about the same time of the year that the nuts fell from the trees.

---

*A group of Anglo-Saxon animal names came to Modern English following exactly the same pattern of change: *picga* to *pigga* to *pig; hocga* to *hogga* to *hog; docga* to *dogga* to *dog; frocga* to *frogga* to *frog; stacga* to *stagga* to *stag*. All of these words are special to English. They were not known, in any form, in other languages.

Chow

In the 1850s, Chinese workers were brought to the Pacific coast of the United States to lay tracks for the new railroad. They took with them their own foods, cooks, and language. The Mandarin Chinese word meaning 'to fry' or 'to cook' is *ch'oa*. We use it now in American English as *chow*, a slang word for food or a meal. We also see it on the menus in Chinese restaurants as *chow mein*, 'cooked noodles'.

Marshmallow

Marshmallows are now made from sugar, water, gelatin, and egg whites. The first marshmallows, eaten almost two thousand years ago, were made from the root of a plant that grew in the marshy waters around the Mediterranean Sea. The Latin word for the plant was *malua*. And, because the *malua* grew in the marshes, *mariscus* in Latin, the plant and the food were both called *marismalua—marshmallow* in English.

Sandwich

John Montague, like many other noblemen of England in the 1700s, liked to gamble. He would have stayed at the gambling tables twenty-four hours at a time—if he hadn't had to leave for meals. One dinnertime, Montague asked that meat be brought to him between two pieces of bread so that he could eat as he gambled. Other noblemen took up the new way of eating and called the food a *sandwich* because John Montague was the Earl of Sandwich.

READING AND WRITING

Read and riddle

The word *read, raeden* in Old English, was not originally used about books, but about magical signs and mystical omens. The meaning of the word *raeden* was 'to guess' or 'to find the meaning of'. People knew very little about natural events and science. They were very superstitious and believed that all events had special meanings for them. If they saw a comet, if a tree branch fell on a windless day, or if a cat walked in front of them, they called the priests to *raeden* the meaning of the event. Something puzzling that had to be explained by the priests was called a *raedels*—the start of our word *riddle*. Anything written on paper or carved on wood was also called a *raedels*, because most of the people could not understand writing and needed to call the priests to *raeden* for them. The priests found the meaning of the letters, just as they found the meaning of the comet, the tree branch, and the cat.

Paper

Our word *paper* comes from *papyrus*, the Latin word for the giant water reed the Egyptians used to make the material on which they wrote. The stem of the reed was cut in strips, soaked in water, pressed smooth, and pasted together into sheets. By the time the word for the sheets had reached Old French, it was *papier*. When the word passed from the French to Middle English, it became *papir*, and by the 1600s could be spelled either *papir* or *paper*.

Pen and Penknife

Pen, spelled *penne* in Middle English and pronounced as two syllables, came from the Latin *penna*, 'feather'. The first pens were made of feathers. Anyone who wanted to use a pen needed a penknife to turn the feather into a pen and sharpen it when it broke or got dull.

Ink

The English word *ink* is a shortened form of a Latin word, *encaustum*, which means 'burn in'. One early method of writing was burning words onto a piece of wood.

Book

In what is now northern Germany, before there was much paper, important information was carved into thin pieces of wood cut from a beech tree. The Old German word for beech tree, *boka*, was first used for the pieces of wood, then for the letters written on them, and later for any writing. When the word reached England in the 1200s, most writing was done on paper, and a *boc* was any sheet of writing or collection of notes.

Paragraph

When the Greeks handwrote their manuscripts, they left no paragraph spaces. There was not much paper, and it was too valuable to waste by leaving spaces. To make it easier for the reader, the Greek writers put a small mark next to the line that started each new subject. The mark was called a *paragraph*, a combination of *para*, 'by the side of', and *graphos*, 'written'. When writers started to leave spaces rather than marks between subjects, they continued to use the word *paragraph*, but it meant all the writing between the spaces.

Quiz

In 1780, the manager of a theatre in Dublin, Ireland, bet that he could bring a new word into the English language in forty-eight hours. He chalked four meaningless letters on walls wherever he could reach all through the city. Soon all Dublin was asking what the letters "q-u-i-z" meant. People said, "It's a practical joke." And the first meaning of *quiz* was 'practical joke'. Later *quiz* took on other meanings—'trick' or 'puzzle', and, especially in the United States, 'test'. (No one can prove that this story is true, but it is known that *quiz* was first heard in Dublin in the spring of 1780. There is no record of the word, in any form, in any language, before that time.)

MONSTERS

These days a *monster* is a strange misshapen creature,
inhuman, weird, and terrible. But in the 16th century, when
the word came to English from the French *monstre*, it had
much of the old Latin meaning—*monstrum*, 'something
marvelous,' 'something to be marveled at'. Over the
centuries, the spelling of the word has changed very little,
but the meaning has changed from something to be
marveled at and admired, to something to be marveled
at and feared—a monster.

Werewolf

In most of Europe and the British Isles during the Middle
Ages, people believed there were men who could turn
themselves into wolves and then back into men again. As
wolves, these men ate the flesh of new corpses and infants
and could only be killed with weapons that had special
charms. In English, such men were called *werewolves*
because *wer* was the Old English word for *man*
(see Man, page 13).

Nightmare
Nightmare is made of two Old English words: *niht,* 'night', and *mare,* from the Old Norse *mara.* The Norse people believed a *mara* was a small but terrible female being that sat on the chest of a sleeping person, stealing his or her breath. During the 13th and 14th centuries, the English used the word *nightmare* to mean this terrible creature. By the end of the 16th century, a *nightmare* had become a bad dream that made you feel as if you could not breathe.

Dragon
In the oldest Greek myths, a winged fire-breathing monster was tied near buried treasure to watch for robbers. The monster was called a *drakon,* from a Greek verb meaning 'to watch for' or 'to see clearly'. Monsters called *drakons* or *dragons* were known in Latin, French, Spanish, German, and Sanskrit. *Dragon* was first used in English in the 13th century. Before then there were probably no dragons in England.

Old Scratch
The Devil is sometimes called *Old Scratch.* He is called this not because he makes us itch, but from an Old Norse word *skratti,* meaning 'monster' or 'wicked one'.

Mummy
The word *mummy* comes from the Arabic *mum,* the name of the liquid wax used to embalm bodies and prepare them for burial.

Gnome
Gnome comes from two Greek words, *geo,* 'earth', and *nomos,* 'dweller'. The name was made up by a 15th-century German writer to describe monsters said to live in the depth of the earth to guard the treasures in mines and quarries. In Scotland such creatures were called *knockers* because if they liked a miner, they were thought to knock on the walls of the mines to show the location of the rich veins of ore.

Elf

An *elf* is a dwarf-sized magic being who has powers to use for good or evil, but who can never be totally trusted. The word, and the creature, have been known almost as long as the English language has been spoken. Elves are seen most often by people who are just awakening or just falling asleep. The Old English elf may have been a relative of the Old German *alf* or *alp*, 'a bad dream creature'.

Goblin

Goblins, noisy demons who live in and around houses, trees, and rivers, are named after a 12th-century French family, the Gobels. The Gobels's house and grounds were filled with spirits who made many strange noises and were the talk of the country. The spirits couldn't have been too frightening, however, because *goblin* is the diminutive (see Glossary, page 61) of Gobel.

Panic

Pan was one of the lesser Greek gods. He was part man, part goat, and all trouble. Unexplained loud noises in the woods were said to be caused by Pan. His sudden appearance, or just the belief that he was nearby, caused terror. People ran screaming from Pan and the terrible trouble he might create. From Pan comes our word *panic*, meaning 'sudden or extreme terror or alarm'.

MYSTERY

Mystery means something hidden, not explained, not fully understood or clearly seen. The English *mystery* came from the Greek word *mysterion*, which came from an earlier Greek word meaning 'to have closed eyes and lips'. When *mysterie* entered English in the 1300s, it had the Greek meaning of a religious truth that is held by faith, but not really understood. Later the word came to mean anything that was not understood.

Clue

A *clue* is a fact or an object that leads to the solution of a mystery. But when *clue*—spelled *clew** until the 1400s—was first used in English, it meant a 'ball of thread'. *Clue* came to English from the Old Dutch *kluwen*, but may be traced back to a Greek word. The Greek word was used for the thread that helped to guide people through the giant maze on the island of Crete. When a clue was found, it was the end of the thread that led out of the maze. So then, as now, a clue was something that helped solve a mystery.

---

* Many words that ended in "ew" in Old and Middle English were changed to end in "ue" when French ways of speaking and spelling increased: *clew* to *clue*; *blew* to *blue*; *trew* to *true*; *hew* (as in color) to *hue*; *dew* to *due*.

Private eye

A *private eye* is a private detective, but the term is not a shortening of *private investigator*. Pinkerton, one of the first and largest detective agencies, had the motto "We never sleep." The motto was printed on cards, posters, and stationery over a drawing of an open *eye*. Private detectives have been called *private eyes* since the 1860s, when Pinkerton started business. The term became especially well known in the 1940s when mystery books with detective heroes became popular.

Fork up

The expression *to fork up* or *to fork out* comes from 17th century English thieves' slang. In the speech of thieves, *fork* was the word for fingers. If you were told to fork out, you were supposed to reach into your pocket with your fingers, pull out your money, and give it to the thieves.

Blackmail

In 16th-century Scotland, *mail* meant 'rent' or 'payment'. Robbers often forced small farmers to pay a second rent in return for protection against fire or other damage. The legal rent, paid in silver, was called *whitemail*. The illegal rent, often paid in cattle or other animals, was called *blackmail*.*

Mafia

The word *mafia*, meaning 'a secret criminal organization', is not an Italian word, but did start in Sicily, a part of Italy. In the 9th century, the Arabs conquered Sicily and the Sicilian families who had fought against them had to find a safe place to hide. The Arabic word for 'a place of safety' was *mafia*, and the Arabs called those who were hidden *the Mafia*. Since the people in hiding came out to attack and rob the Arab invaders, *mafia* came to mean an organized band of thieves.

*The mail the postman brings got its name from the French word *malle*, a bag in which letters were carried.

Bully

The word *bully*, a person who picks on weaker people, comes not from the word *bull*, but from an Old Dutch word *boel*. *Boel* meant 'lover' in Dutch, as it did at first in English. Slowly *bulle* changed to mean a 'fine fellow' and then a 'showoff'. Finally in the 17th century, as now, a bully became a person who shows off by hitting the weak. In England *bully* is still sometimes used to mean a fine person or thing.

Phoney

Phoney, meaning 'fake' or 'insincere', comes from British and American underworld slang. Tricksters called an imitation gold ring, which was sold to a sucker as real gold, a *fawney*. Around 1920, when the word started to be used by honest people to mean a fake of any type, the word's spelling was changed to look like a Greek word, starting with "ph". Maybe people thought the "ph" made it look phancier.

Jury

Jury, the term for the twelve people who judge innocence or guilt in a trial, comes from the Latin word *juro*, meaning 'I swear'. When jury trials started in England in the 1300s, each man answered "juro" to questions about his ability and willingness to judge honestly.

Prison and Jail

Prison came to English in the 11th century with the Old French language of the Norman invaders. The word started as the Latin *prehendere*, meaning 'to seize' or 'to hold'. The same Latin word is the root of the English word *apprehend*, 'to arrest'.

Jail comes from the Latin word *caveola*, meaning 'little cave' or 'cage'. Over the centuries the Romans changed the spelling to *caviola* and the Spanish to *gaiola*. The Normans brought the word to England as *gaole*, although it was sometimes spelled *jaiole*. *Gaol*, pronounced as *jail* is, was used in colonial America and is still used in England. *Jail* became the popular spelling in the United States in the 1800s.

GLOSSARY

Roots

Often a new English word grows out of an already existing word. The original words, usually in slightly different forms than when used alone, are called *root words*. They are often from Greek and Latin, but they don't have to be. The root words make up the basic, most important part of the new word. The root of our word *animal* is from the Latin word *anima*, 'breath of life'. Someone who talks in a lively way is called *animated*. Bringing a cartoon character to life in movies is called *animation*. If you can recognize a word root, you can sometimes figure out the meaning of an unfamiliar word.

The Latin word *scribo* means 'write'. The root is in the English words *script, scribble, scriptures, postscript*. The Greek word for 'write' or 'draw' is *grapho*; as an English root it is usually *graph* or *gram*. A *grammar* book gives the rules of the written language. Many words are made of two root words. The Greek root *gram* is paired with the Greek word for 'far', *tele*, to make *telegram*, 'far writing'. *Graph* is paired with the Greek word for 'light', *phot*, to make *photograph*, 'light writing'.

Prefix

The word *prefix* is a good example of what prefixes are and how they are used. *Fix*, the root, comes from the Latin *ficura*, 'place' or 'fasten'. *Pre-*, from the Latin *prae-*, means 'before'. A prefix is a syllable never used alone that is 'placed before' a root word. The prefix changes or adds to the meaning of the root word. If you *view* a movie, you *see* it. If you *preview* a movie, you see it before other people can.

Many different words can be formed by adding different prefixes to a single root. *Porto* is the Latin for 'carry'; as a root it is usually *port*. The addition of prefixes gives *deport*, 'carry away'; *export*, 'carry out or carry from'; *import*, 'carry in'; *report*, 'carry back'; *support*, 'carry or hold from below'; *transport*, 'carry across or through'. More than one prefix can be added to the same root at the same time, as in *un-sup*-ported, 'not carried from below'.

Suffix

In the word *suffix*, the root *fix*, 'place' or 'fasten', is combined with the prefix *sub-*, used as *suf-*, 'after'. Suffixes are syllables that cannot stand alone and that are 'placed after' the root. The addition of a suffix changes the meaning of a root in less important ways than the addition of a prefix. A suffix, however, can change a word into a different part of speech. The suffix -er means 'one who'. When it is added to the verb *dance*, it makes *dancer*, 'one who dances', a noun.

There are many more suffixes than prefixes, and their meanings are often not as exact. The suffix -er is one of the most common, and it can be used in at least six different ways. The most common use is as 'one who'; *port* means 'carry', a *porter* is 'one who carries'. But -er is also often used as a comparative, as in *nice, nicer*. Another common suffix is -able; *portable* means 'able to be carried'.

More than one suffix can be added to a root at the same time. *Joyful* means 'full of joy'; *joy-ful-ness* means 'the state of being full of joy'. And a root can have both prefix and suffix added to it. A *transporter* is 'one who carries through'. Suffixes and prefixes can be used with all roots, whether or not they are from the Greek and Latin.

Diminutive

We say *Billy* for *Bill*, *Ruthie* for *Ruth*, *horsie* for *horse*, *dolly* for *doll*. All these words are called *diminutives*. A *diminutive* is a form of a word that shows a small size or feeling of familiarity or affection. A word is usually made into a diminutive by the addition of a suffix, most often -y or -ie. Words can also be made into diminutives by adding -let or -ling. A book*let* is a 'small book', a duck*ling* is a 'little duck'.

Some suffixes are no longer used to form diminutives, but words made from them are still part of English. The Old French used -et and -ette to form the diminutive and gave us pock*et* (see page 23), targ*et* (see page 36), and jack*et* (see page 23). The French still form their diminutives with -et and -ette, but the endings are less common in English. Din*ette*, 'small dining room', and cigar*ette*, 'small cigar', are among the few modern uses. The Middle English used -kin and -kins as diminutives, but these have mostly gone out of use, except in a few stray words such as baby*kins* and bump*kin*, the strange exclamation 'Odds Bod*kins*', and some family names that started as diminutive nicknames. Dic*kins*, Jen*kins*, and Wil*kins* once meant 'little Dick', 'little John or Jean', and 'little Will'.

INDEX

Hello and Goodby

Until the 1800s, English-speaking people didn't use *hello* as a greeting. They said "good day" or "good evening" or "how do you do?" In the early 1600s, *hallo* was a meaningless sound used on land and at sea to get someone's attention. It may have developed on its own in England, or it may have come from the French attention-getting phrase *ho la*, meaning 'hey there'. The word could be heard over long distances and could easily be shouted. After two centuries of shouting *hallo* at a distance, people started to say *hallo*, and then *hello*, to each other when they passed on the street. Now *hello* is the usual English greeting.

Goodby started as the phrase *God be with you*. The phrase was slurred, or contracted, to *God be wy you* and then *God bwye*, as it was spelled and said when the Pilgrims left for the New World. By the middle 1600s, the word changed to good-bye or goodby, perhaps to go with the earlier phrases "good day" and "good evening."* In the 1600s, people also said, when parting, "So long as we are parted may you be well." That long phrase was shortened to our present-day *so long*.

*Some etymologists (people who study words) think that *God bwye* changed to *goodby* because people did not want to use the name of God in everyday speech. Many of our words started as substitutes for religious words. *Gosh* and *golly* were both 1740s substitutes for *God*; *good grief*, a substitute for *good God*. *Gee* and *jeepers* started as substitutes for *Jesus*; *heck* was a substitute for *hell*; *drat*, *dang*, and *darn* were substitutes for *damn*.